WHY DO CAMELS

Have Such Long Eyelashes?

A BOOK ABOUT DESERT ANIMALS

Written by Jack Beard Illustrated by Jayri Gómez

Have you ever wondered WHY desert animals do the things they do?

Deserts are home to lots of interesting animals that are fun to see and even more fun to learn about. Each of these animals has special traits that help them to live and thrive in the desert.

sun

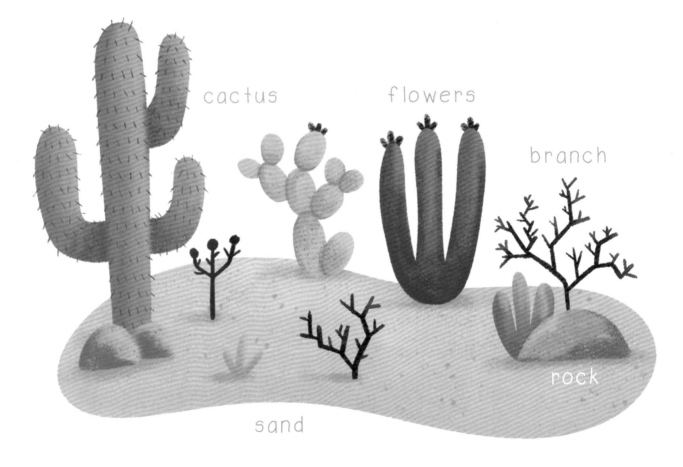

cactus

flowers

branch

rock

sand

star

sand dune

sun

Can you find the shapes hiding in the shadows?

Why do RATTLESNAKES RATTLE?

Is it so they can JOIN A BAND
with their desert animal friends?

Rattlesnakes rattle as a warning! When a rattlesnake feels threatened, they shake their tail really fast to make a loud rattling sound. This lets animals know a rattlesnake is near and to keep their distance.

head

eye

rattle

tongue

tail

body

meerkats

scales

lizard

tracks

shell

Can you slither
around like
a snake?

Why do FENNEC FOXES have BIG ears?

ears

plant

tail

Is it so they can LISTEN IN ON other animals' CONVERSATIONS?

tortoise

fennec fox

What color is the teacup?

rock

Fennec foxes use their big ears to help them hear small animals and insects as they move around the desert.

Use your ears like a fennec fox! What can you hear outside your window?

brush

ground

Their ears also help to keep them
cool in the hot desert sun.

sun

cactus

Is it because they are the ONLY DESERT
ANIMALS without a BLANKET?

head

Lizards are cold-blooded animals, which means they cannot control their own body temperature.

What color is the lizard's hoodie?

tail

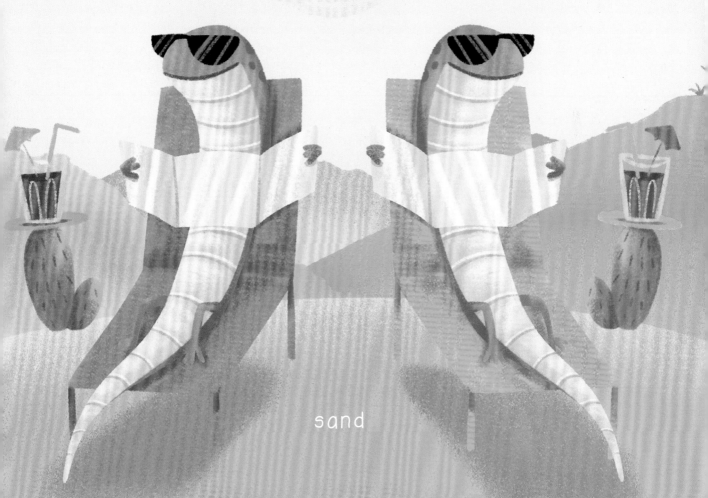

sun

sky

sand

Instead of using a blanket, lizards sunbathe during the day and often huddle together in burrows at night to stay warm.

Why do coyotes HOWL at NIGHT?

Is it because they are AFRAID OF THE DARK?

moon

coyote

hills

cactus

Can you howl
like a coyote?

sand

Coyotes aren't afraid of the dark. They are active both during the day and at night. Coyotes mainly howl at night to communicate with other coyotes. They also howl to let other animals know that this is their territory and they should back off!

tree
tumbleweed
rock
Can you spot the lizard hiding behind the plant?

Why do TORTOISES have SHELLS?

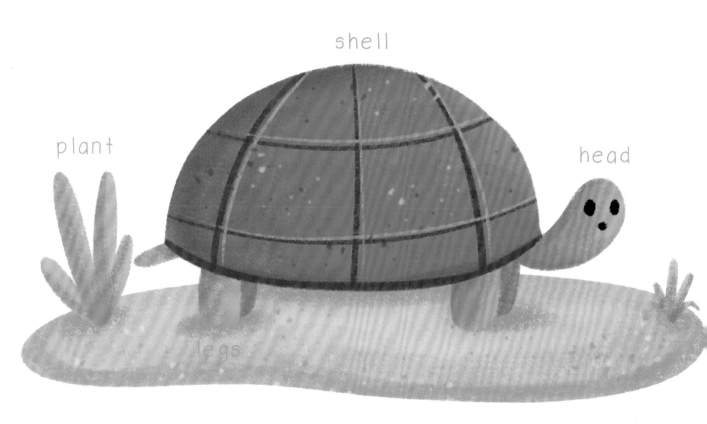

Is it so they can always WIN
in a game of HIDE-AND-SEEK?

fennec fox

snake

lizard

grass

tortoise

How many
different animals
do you see?

If a tortoise is in danger or just feels scared, it can quickly pull its head, legs, and tail inside its shell to hide. A tortoise's shell is like a special house that keeps them safe and comfortable. It even grows with them throughout their life.

Is it because they're wearing MAKEUP?

Camels naturally have long eyelashes! On windy desert days the sand can blow up into big clouds of dust. When that happens, a camel's long eyelashes act as a filter, keeping the scratchy sand from getting in their eyes. Their eyelashes also protect their eyes from the sun.

wind

nose

cactus

sun

Count the camels and their humps!
1   2

camels

tumbleweed

brush

lizard

WHAT ELSE CAN DESERT ANIMALS DO?

There is so much to learn about animals in the desert.
Read more about each one here!

RATTLESNAKE

Rattlesnakes can grow up to 8 feet long.

Baby rattlesnakes are born without rattles.

FENNEC FOX

Fennec foxes are sometimes called desert foxes.

Fennec foxes can live without water for long periods of time.

Fennec foxes are the smallest foxes in the world.

MEERKAT

A group of meerkats
is called a mob.

Meerkats live together
in underground burrows.

Meerkats use their tails
for balance when they
stand on their hind legs
(which they do a lot).

TORTOISE

A tortoise is a type of reptile.

Unlike turtles, tortoises can't swim.

Some tortoises can live to be over 100 years old.

COYOTE

Coyotes are members of the dog family.

Coyotes hunt for food in small family groups or alone.

Baby coyotes are called pups.

LIZARD

There are many species of lizards that live in the desert including the desert iguana.

Some desert lizards can absorb water through their skin.

CAMEL

A camel's hump doesn't store water. It actually stores fat.

Camels are born without humps.

There are two types of camels. One type has one hump and the other type has two humps.